BROKEN

by Jason Wallace

Copyright © 2018 by Jason Wallace
All rights reserved. This book or any portion thereof may not be reproduced or used in any manner whatsoever without the express written permission of the publisher except for the use of brief quotations in a book review.
Printed in the United States of America

First Printing, 2018

ISBN 978-0-9979678-6-9

A Digital Mess Productions
P.O. Box 4005
New York, NY 10163

Dedicated To:

The one great love even

Nina dreamed about...

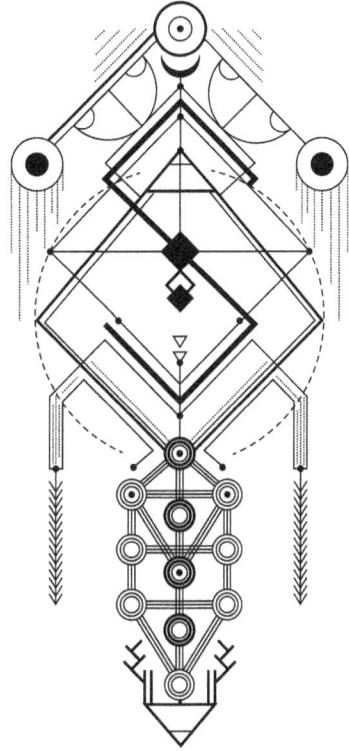

Foreword

Everything you mentally digest is equally as crucial as the things you eat. From TV to books to the noises you hear outside your window; however, nothing is more important to your mental diet than your communication with other people. Surround yourself with people like Jason Wallace, who from my experience, is someone who isn't afraid to speak his truth, but who is non-judgmental, and always reciprocates the energy you pour into any interaction. The world needs more people like Jason, and it's not only an honor that I have the opportunity to contribute to his art but more importantly, share a bond with a man who is of sound principle.

- Al Patron

Forgive Me

For the pain I caused

For my immaturity

For the dumb mistakes

For my insecurity

For not elevating you

For not valuing our love

For chasing butterflies

For making you second guess yourself

For wasted time

For broken promises

For not saying these words sooner

My Blanket

I lost my blanket last night

Mommy said she hasn't seen it, and it's around

But it's no where to be seen

I grew up with that blanket

Holding it close before I even knew what it was

Loving before I knew I had such a capacity

Everywhere I went, my blanket came too

Keeping me warm, protecting me, giving me something to grab hold of

During those nights when the dark was too much

When the wind laughed at my fright

And now it's gone

Could it be hiding under the bed, playing a bad joke on me?

Did it unravel under the pressure a precocious little girl would exert?

How am I supposed to fall asleep again?

What's going to insure my safety?

How can I trust another blanket to not disappear on me?

Mommy's crying for some reason

I think she lost her blanket too.

Bad Investment

How could I have mistaken you for the woman of my dreams?

I guess my mind & heart conspired to teach me a lesson on my own personal worth

For too long I undervalued myself, believing what I got was just compensation for what I gave

Had I looked closely at the ledger, I would have seen the bleeding ink

I would have recognized the signs of a bankrupt relationship

The stock I brought because you said our relationship would only get better

You exaggerated to make me buy more, while you sold incrementally

Maybe I should've consulted someone

But at times you feel embarrassed about these things

You feel you can't trust a stranger

Had I heeded my own counsel, my losses may not have been as great

I now cash out at a loss

Thankfully no one else was brought into this emotional Enron

I'll leave the investigation for the powers that be ore I'm worn out by your Thotopoly

Thankfully, my love is like money, my heart a generous benefactor

The more you give, the more comes back

Thankfully, I've divested myself of you.

Leave Me Alone

Ignorant Bastard!

How many times must I tell your stupid ass to stop calling?

When are you going to stop leaving those sorry messages on my voicemail

Begging me for one more chance

Why?

So you can fuck me mentally all over again?

So you can TRY to pleasure me?

I gave you the D-Game because your limp dick wasn't worth the effort

This text isn't worth the effort either

I just felt like getting something off my chest

Clear my mind, so when my new man comes over, he'll have my undivided attention.

That's him now.

Beat it.

Caught

Once I was able to fly
Soaring through the clouds like an eagle
Coasting on a mild summer breeze

Once I was like a lion
Strong and in control of my today and tomorrow
Protecting my ground while gaining more

Once i was like the sea
Filled with so much life and energy
Flowing from one port to the next

But I no longer fly
My wings bound
A burden keeps me on the ground

I no longer roam
I am caged against my will
Losing more ground each setting sun

I can no longer swim
The water has turned to quicksand
Every movement sinks me deeper into the abyss

I can never return to who I was
Life's paths lead in a new direction
I can only hope that our lives together
Will take us to a place of fulfillment

Walls Talk

If I could talk to your walls
what would I say?
how would I make them bend and sway
move to my words and yield their prize
it's a delicate proposition
well, that's what I surmise
should I whisper sweet nothings
warming up the foundation
or should I shout at the top of my lungs
a worthy vociferous proclamation
would your walls open up
or would they grow taller yet still
would they keep you enclosed
or will they bend to my will
the fragrance of your perfume
waffles through and silently sings
making me desperate, restless
this isolation continuously stings
I need them to speak
I need to know my struggle is valid
I need to hear your words
I need your walls to come down
I need you

Pain

The pain of joy is when it leaves, and there's nothing you can do about it

The pain of hope is when it's lost, stuck in a forest of despair, the quicksand of depression

The pain of love is everyday taking your soul and ounce at a time

The pain of life is death, not knowing when it's coming to end all pain..

Broken

How did this start between me and you?
Is it the imagery
Or the reality of what I know is true?
You came in my life when I was down and out
And made smile again
We shared intimacies
Like grandma's recipes
As if we were old friends
This is why I need to know
Why did you leave?
Where you tired of me?
Did my touch darken your soul?
This is hurting me
No, you can't come back to me
You need to learn control
How many times can I say I fell
Before the whispers start?
How many times must I feel your belt
Before my body falls apart
Can't you see?
You're killing me
All in the name of love
I never disrespected
Or even acted reckless
But my actions you still judge
You used to be kind
Opened all my doors even rubbed my back
Now you kick me
Tell me I'm nothin without you
And every word I say is greeted with a smack
I used to love you
Now I wish you'd die
So I can live again
I just can't believe
The man of my dreams
Turned into a nightmare

Clarity

I want to apologize for not being the perfect man you've
been looking for to reside in your perfect world
The place where you seem to always be right
The place where your charming attitude devours one's self-confidence outright
Realization has come too late
As I have discovered you are nothing more than a selfish little girl
Self-absorbed in the mirror of your life, not realizing
The glass is transparent
The world can see you for who you truly are
Since your M.O. has become painfully apparent
It's been difficult for me to sincerely love you
Due to the sarcastic comments you so masterfully hurl
My friends told me you were a spiteful bitch
But I defended your honor without hook or hitch
Now it seems you've become recluse
Shut tight like an oyster without a pearl
Worthless to all but yourself in the end
I honestly don't think I could stand to be your friend
Still, you have a nice life and don't ever call me again...

Heart Cries

I can't tell you how many times I wanted to cry
How many times I shook my head and asked God why
When I saw that man begging on the train

Is there a mystery at work here
Is this proof that God is not really there
The situation causes my heart to strain

The shelters are full but will let him in
But foolish pride keeps help from him
Even at our lowest we are at our worst

The drug use has weakened the mind of this once great nation
Cutting short the lifespan of a once promising generation
Drying up the well of thought creating an unenviable thirst

Children being coveted as sexual pawns
Fathers and mothers neglecting their daughters and sons
Families no longer exist as we know it
Television has become our greatest teacher
Replacing the parents, relatives and preacher
Deciding if it makes dollars then show it

My heart hurts as I witness death
My mind struggles to find what's left
Are these the last days of society

We need God to end this devilry
To awaken us from our drunken revelry
And infuse us with love and sobriety

For my daughter to have a better life
I'll have to make that sacrifice
And give her all the tools to succeed

But even with all my love and care
I can only hope to lead her there
She will have to realize her own dreams

The Ugly

The prototype of women, you stepped from a wet dream

A gift from God because no man could ever achieve such magnificent perfection

Your eyes hold a kinetic quality as if looking into a rainbow

Your hair flows like a waterfall down to the small of your delicately arched back

Your legs, so long and slender, could enrapt me for time eternal

The shape of your hips dictates only a real man may enter your bountiful garden

Your bosom brings comfort and security to the wildest of man

Your eyes meet mine, and lock. dancing with anticipation of our first words

Your hands fold and refold, searching for some comfort

Your lips purse, wet with delight as I approach

I nod to begin our dance, but then the music stops,

The band leaves as I do too

What happened to my sweet angel?

What could make me forsake such a woman, who's mere smile could make one reach an inner happiness?

What could keep me from such sweet delights known only to a lucky few?

She lit a cigarette...

Shattered Trust

Should I have cried when you slept with my friend because he satisfied your urges, which are indispensable?
Should I have died when you persisted to see him because you liked the feel of his always accommodating genitals?
My love went beyond the bullshit that you seem to constantly engulf us in.
My love is unable to respond to your lusty ways and unforgettable sins.
I've made many moves to patch things up, but you just laugh at all my ideas.
I've never lost my cool in the heat of it all, even though this seems so surreal.
You made me believe the long search was over and my find was my greatest achievement.
You made me conceive a notion in my mind of a woman with out malice or bereavement.
And what should I do about you my friend, my comrade through life's never-ending pursuit.
Of her I guess I should have expected as much, but to me your actions don't compute.
On that fateful day we bonded for life I knew I had found me a brother.
Like MJ or Magic, Larry or Oscar, your style was unlike any other.
Though different in spirit, we always thought alike.
And I guess when it's said and done we even seemed to love alike.
It seems women are a different story since their seduction comes from many an unseen angle.
You ultimately gave into her temptations and started a Jerry Springer love triangle.
With her I'm just upset and with time my anger shall subside and pass.
But with you I'm disappointed because destroyed our bond for some ass.
It may never be the same with us, but I guess time heals all deep scarring wounds.
I just hope you guys are happy and paid because the baby make her entrance in June.

Cloudy Skies

Clear skies cloud my mind as thoughts turn to the day you left

It was a good time to be alive as we knew our futures were intertwined

A wish became a dream, a dream became hope

But hope disappeared as you abandoned it in favor of despair

There was something in your mind which kept you a prisoner of fear

What, I don't know til this day

But it commanded your heart and body, even as your soul struggled to be set free

I can remember the phone call as I looked out at the sky, as you looked out too

But you was at a point you felt was closer to God, and I was nowhere near you

You told me how good I made you feel, how alive you were on this day

How your heart beat 1000 times a second knowing I was looking at the same sky as you

You made me promise to never forget, how we smiled when we kissed

To remember our life together as stronger than the eternity we will spend apart

And then you left

Causing me to find some solace in the memory of what was my personal Eden

But how can what was sustain me for the rest of my days?

How can yesterday do more for me tomorrow, when I need a hug today?

You left me confused, fore how could you yearn for me to be your knight, your ray of lite in the dark void

If you knew your destination was one you couldn't be saved from

why did I invest my love and time only to be left bankrupt and overdrawn?

The sun shines brightly, the sky a clear blue sea

I just hope you've found your peace

And from heaven, you smile down on me

Allow Me To Live

Every night before I go to sleep
I think about what it would be like
If I died before my dream came true

If I could never hold you in my arms
Never make you smile
Never tell you I love you

Would the Lord do such a thing
After awakening my soul
Just to summon me to his side

Does such cruel irony exist
In a world of fate and faith
I hope to never know such a trial

How sad would we be
After reaching a place of joy
Our own personal Eden

I could not watch you from above
A dreary soul in paradise am I
A celestial body whose spirit broken and beaten

I thank the Lord each morning I arise
That I am alive and well in this land of peace
My land of promise and faith

I pray that we can share many a sunrise
Becoming two of one
Man, Woman, and hopefully child on the way

When I close my eyes
I see you smiling at me
The happiest you have ever been

But if I should die and rise to heaven
For your love
I would live again

A Kiss

A kiss from you is needed right now

My reserves are very low

And need replenishing

The good fortitude I possess weakens

As the touch from your delicate lips fades

Into memory

I need to find you before I faint

From the lack of affection

Even as I write, my head feels dizzy

The doctor can't prescribe the remedy this time

Only a kiss from you will do.

Daydream

Sleep is an estranged lover

She barely comes to me though I call and plead to her

There was a time when we were dynamic and bound

I could rely on her to restore my energies

Lately, it's as if she's found a new muse

Leaving me a weary, restless soul

So I sing, I let the music soothe me, overcoming my body and soul

And immersing me into the tunes

The tones

The boom boom boom of the bass

The high hat and the sexy seduction of the saxophone

I sing because my entire being requires it

I sing because if I stop

I will surely die....

Great One

There she is

The myth/dream/legend floating in your mind

She's materialized

A rare beauty she is

Walking confidently among the masses

Gracefully making her presence felt

A Great One

She comes along when the odds are against you

When you don't think you're at the top of your game

But you want her

What do you do?

Take a chance or let the moment pass?

Step up or remain on the bench?

You may never know what could have been

You will know that you let her get away

A Great One

A sistah who takes the air out of you

A woman who lights up a room when she enters

The vixen who let's you know what she wants by the look in her eyes

A lady who never disrespects you

But you may never know

Why?

Because she's gone

Down The River

Drifting down the river, I saw you

Pretty as can be, rowing your boat with the force of a hurricane

Yet you only went in circles

I amused myself as others offered to help you

Amused at the help you'd have to provide in return

Me, I paddled up next to you

Dove in the water and set your rudder straight

You said thanks and started to row again

An again you didn't move

People on the banks snickered, and called to you

Said I was the biggest huckster of em all

You looked me in my eyes, gave me an oar, and asked that I row

Asked that I help you get to where you wanted to go

I was curious as to your destination and anxious to see what adventures lay ahead

So I took an oar, and together we began our journey

Sigmatic

Simple eloquence can not explain these here images

Invoking digital 'glyphics like the ones lining the pyramids

Gassed on the fact my PS renders executive quality graphics

Making you delete .psd's cuz your shyt's were MS Paint wackness

Announcing the new style to complement my artful floetry

Tellin tales and wreckin tails combining sigs with soulful poetry

Imagehost holds me down so my joints load a little faster

Creativity on a higher level ,I'll never settle even after I'm a Master

F.O.C.U.S.

For me to be at this point in life

On the verge of greatness, yet stuck in mediocrity

Causes my soul to reach out to God

Unclear where my heartstrings stretch to find him

Searching inward for the answer..

Sunday Morning

I had to curb my enthusiasm

Early one Sunday morning

Because the need to hear the delicate tenor of your voice was overwhelming

I fought the feeling, deciding to wait for the right time

The time when the power of your voice is at its' peak

But in my heart, anytime is the right time

Fore when you speak to someone you care for

The words go to directly to the heart

Travel thru the soul and reach the brain

All in the time it takes for your lips to press against mine

I'll wait until noon to dial your number on my cell

But I'm sending you instant messages from my heart so you can dream of me..

Fresh Start Vol. 2

I reneged on my resolutions and reinforced my resolve

I realized your smile reached parts of me that needed recharging

Remarkably I'm calm, but that's because you reside outside my present

Realistically, I'd be eager to reengage our conversation

Reconnect on multiple levels

Readjust my mind and body to accommodate your pleasant presence

I reckon you're smiling right now, because you know you were resigned to have a good year, not remembering how you ended the last

You reached me at a good time, as I have rediscovered why women are so wonderful

I've researched my heart and soul and I've come up with positive results

I've relinquished my hold on loneliness and wrestled hope from the jaws of despair

I found you..

Inspired

You inspire me to greatness

Not an easy feat as I my determination and drive are God-given

Could it be, that you are his messenger?

Sent to take me that extra mile past satisfaction

To squelch the fire raging in my belly

Or to ignite a new one in my heart?

Either way, your presence is more than welcome

For I have spent too many days alone

Days pondering about things such as this contrite little soliloquy of love

Do we mambo to the rhythm of my heart beat

Or do we waltz to the jazz in your eyes

Clearly you've struck a well guarded chord within me

Reaching the one part of my soul no one knew existed

But you.

I Wonder

Sometimes I look out on other people and I wonder
What is your life like
Do you know happiness and joy
Pain and misery
Are your dreams fulfilled or washed away like sandcastles on a beach
Can you make it through the day without crying because your heart hurts
Or do smiles reside permanently on your face
I want to ask these questions of strangers so they will become familiar to me
Anonymous faces in a crowd, living synonymous lives to mine
I want to hear your story.

When I'm Alone

when I'm alone

I think of ways to reach you

inspire you

complete you

I need my time and space

to clear a path through time and space

the words seek out your soul and zip through your being

returning to me like a warm zephyr off the Pacific

in the end I inspire you

but the reality is, you've inspired you

I'm just the messenger

transcribing your inner thoughts

working away

all alone...

The Parable

My intellectual advancement is exceeded only by the emotional gains I have tried to achieve day by day, in hopes of combining my heart and mind to my soul and sparking the fierce fires of my spirit which have been slowly dying out due in part to neglect with a healthy dose of betrayal at the hands of someone I once loved with my heart everything who now I realize never loved me quite the same way due to the incompatibilities of our life energies which differed in both sum and substance to the point of being not polar opposites but instead unlikely allies in the creation of the one who I know will love me unconditionally with a smile that let's me know it's finally okay to trust a woman with my heart..

United & Strong

I think you're someone I need in my life

In some form

In some way

My heart beats faster around you

My ears listen for the sweet melody of your voice

My hands tingle when I think of caressing your silky skin

It was said we couldn't be together

We shouldn't be together

But look at us now

Us

United and Strong

Thoughts

Dreams smothered by the dirty blanket of despair

Hope washed away like the sandcastles I built as a child

Vision never seems to focus

Obscured and

It's impossible to move forward when you're stuck in a mental quicksand

It's there when it's not and gone again

Feel like swimming to a distant land

But every stroke I take brings me closer to the shores I'm trying to escape

There's no love or like, no feelings holding my heart hostage

Just something I can't put my finger on...

I Wish

I wish you would wake up from the nightmare you envision

I wish you would let me in

I wish you wouldn't push so hard

I wish we could become more than friends

I wish you didn't know so much pain and struggle

I wish there was some light in your life

I wish you would believe I am your protector

I wish you dreamed of being my wife

I wish you would hold my hand

I wish we could live as one

I wish you realized I'm your rock

I wish we could go back to having fun

I wish these things because my heart needs them

I wish these things because my soul is incomplete

I wish these things with the hope to actualize

I wish these things because I need you.

Damn

There's no way I could've known I was to meet you

No way to know I could never be with you

Had I known what possibilities life had to offer, I would have acted differently

Walked that solitary road until our paths crossed

I would have made it my goal to get us on a path together

Because life is really living when you have someone to walk with…

The Walls

The walls are my guardians

Holding my secrets tight

Silent

Strong

Absorbing all

Releasing none

When it's dark and the door's closed

When I'm creating prophetic prose

When the words enlighten me

The walls know

The similes and haikus bounce off the walls

Like digital Pong, but none escape

Because the walls have pledged allegiance to the literature

An oath sworn on the tome of the Bard

To protect me and my musings

To nurture me in my cocoon

The walls guard my Soul

Because that's what I pour into these lines

Should they fall and crumble

Then so shall I...

!nternet L@ve

It's time I changed OS's

As a matter of fact, hardware too

The machine I had is outdated

A plain beige dinosaur I brought back in 2002

It came with plenty of software

But I quickly found out the programs were of little use to me.

I tried to upgrade, but the OS would freeze up on me

I tried to get new drivers, even asking for some tech help

But the damn thing wouldn't take the new code

I resigned myself to puddling along with a machine that didn't suit me

A machine that had a mind of it's own.

It's like I had Blaster, SoBig, and MyDoom all rolled into one

A nasty virus infecting every folder it came across

A worm, planted deep within, unknown to me

Eating away at the bytes, causing severe damage until it was too late

I had to shut it down, remove the power and box it up

All the accessories need to go too

As I figure I'll go to a new platform

A new way of thinking because that Window is closed.

Pride & Prejudice

A lonely and tormented soul

I meander through life with one goal in sight

Death

I've made it this far traveling down my paths

Sometimes with cheery company

But usually alone

Everything I achieved is due to my greatness

No one helped me rise from the slums to be lord of the flies

Only the late night company of a young lass or two slowed me down

Re-energized my drive for perfection

I shed my family long ago

As the journey is much easier with no one hanging on your neck

Do they love me?

Who cares?!?

Just know that I made them who they are today

I made me who I am today

As time comes to collect its due

As the road of my life grows ever shorter

Know that I outlived them all

My friends and foes

At my funeral, don't cry for me

Just smile and say:

"He was an arrogant bastard but he was a successful one"

Memory

I felt the sun on my face, and I thought of you touching me
I felt the light breeze and thought of you kissing words to me

I saw the clear blue sky and thought of those pretty brown eyes

All I know around me is you

I heard the sweet birds sing

And knew you were calling me

I saw your face in the clouds and it was a sight to see

I smelled a rose in the air and thought you was standing there

Everything around me is you

I taste the honey of your kiss when I go to eat

I smell the scent that's only you in my shirts and tees

I feel your loss more than ever cause I love you baby

I need it all around to be you

Train Ride

I travel the city

Or rather beneath the city

Alone with thousands of others

Not daring to share my journey

Afraid to make contact with someone

On the same path as I

What brings this about?

True fear, or lack of social tact?

A profound respect

For subway rider etiquette?

More like a disconnect

Some people we see everyday

Sharing with them time and space

While too afraid to look at their face

And at the hint of an eye we look away

I ride the train to get where I'm going

But I enjoy the journey just the same

Time to reflect on where I've been

Time to decide where I'm going.

Protection

I've come to the point where I know I want you in my life.

It's taken considerable prayer, pain, and trust in myself to realize

Yours is the voice I need to hear each morning when the sun shines brightly on a new day.

Do you feel the same way?

Do you care for me enough to stay?

Can our union transcend the physicality, embrace the spirituality, and reach an emotional equality

Only two people truly in love know?

I ask these questions trying to discern whether your answers will come from your mind or your heart.

The latter means it's only a matter of time before I can finally open up.

The former dooms us to the merry go round of 'What Ifs'

It's time I moved myself out of the line of emotional fire.

Retreat from the front and decide whether to evacuate or hold the line.

Not an easy decision to make, but who said Life was easy?

Library

As I look out across the platform
Waiting for the Downtown Express
A curiosity has overcome me.
Looking at each person's face as they anxiously await the iron horse to carry them home
I realize my location
Not satisfied with my discovery, I board my own weapon of mass transit
Where more of the same awaits
People
Dressed up and down
Covering an array of colors
Some thin, while others thick
But everyone is ultimately the same
You and I my friend, my faithful companion on this journey called Life
We reside in a Library
For you see, each of God's children has so many stories residing in them
Chapters dedicated to this or that combined in the form of a Novel
Everyday the Sun shines on your face, a new page has begun, with your soul providing the ink.
Each night with the Moon high above, a page comes to an end, waiting for tomorrow's adventures to begin the story again.
The Great Librarian
She keeps all her books in order, deciding when each are due.
Replacing old worn out books with brand new ones
Sometimes she'll let a book go past the date of return
Because the story is too good to end so soon
Other times she'll cut it short, leaving an unfinished story with a message inside.
I share my personal pages with you, as I enjoy your good company
I share my life with you as I hope you'll remember me when you write your own stories.
Happy Reading..

Relations

I knew

I lied

You covered

You tried

I forgive

I moved

You regressed

You continued

I tired

I left

You realized

I'm the best

Too late

Too bad

I'm refreshed

And too glad

A Perfect Day

A perfect day would be waking up next to you.
Energized by a morning kiss to go conquer the world.

A perfect day would move so fast while we're apart
And slow down when we're together.

A perfect day would be getting lost in your eyes
And seeing the true beauty that is your soul.

A perfect day hasn't come yet, but I'm praying it will.
I'm praying for you...

love jones

Girl, you move me

You put me in a sentimental mood like Nina's poem

I can't get enough of your love

It's the sweetest thing in the world

Makes me wanna rush over and taste your jelly

Groove a little sumthin' sumthin' with you

I'll be your brother to the night

Hopelessly in love with you

Let's make love in the rain and laugh until the sun rises.

If you could see inside my heart, inside my love, you'd see I was happy and whole.

This thing we got is special and I like it.

I got a love jones for you…

I Promise

It's not the easiest thing

Protecting something so rare and special
Realizing that it could only happen once
Only makes it that much more appreciated
Makes it that much more rewarding
If only to those two people involved
Seen by others as dancing a private waltz
Envied by those wishing they could hear our sweet song

Tell me your greatest fears
Only if you want me to vanquish them

Lose yourself inside my ebony
Only if you trust me unconditionally
Vacate the past and let's make our future
Enough talkin' bout it, let's be it

Yesterday was the end of the beginning
Only a bright tomorrow awaits us...
Us.

5 Things

I've acquired many items on my journey through life
Keeping mementos of past success and failure
Discarding the things I felt indifferent about
In the body though, it's different
My soul is the true collector
It stores the love I've received in my heart
Love gained through new and joyous relationships
Love found when none was in sight
Love held as a hostage in the war between man and woman
Love given unconditionally
The hunger can be found in my stomach
The hunger to be the best
The hunger and desire to strive to the highest level
The hunger felt when the job is not done right and no one eats
I feel the nakedness in my eyes
I see the world as it sees me
And I'm humbled by the images
All the smiles and laughs stripped away to expose the truth
The real me, the me that's real
The me you think is real
The me you need to feel
The poverty courses through my blood
Constantly reminding me of the roots which have given me my solid foundation
The poverty I try to leave yet allow to reside in me like a symbiote
Living freely, giving me the strength to carry on
Hard labor carves the lines my hands
Making them sinewy strong and resilient
Many years have I toiled
Giving my hands no rest for they know no other way than to toil and traffic in power and pain
When I lay down for my final rest
Five things accumulate inside you: love, poverty, hunger, nakedness, hard labor

Conversation of Heroes

Brother Malcolm I say
What's the word today?
Have the people decided to rise up?

Not yet Doctor King
Seems like it's the same damn thing
So many sheep and not enough leaders

What happened to the BlackPanthers
Has that group been dismantled
Black people as a whole need to wizen up

Well from my point of view
Malcolm, the numbers are askew
The disillusioned far outweigh the believers

Is this the cause we died for
To see our women wronged
And the men folk caught up in drugs

See Martin I thought we had won
But when your leaders die by the gun
It makes that part of culture alright

How had we lived to finish our work
And joined forces while on earth
We'd have a nation of men, proud & strong

Jews, Christians and Muslims united
And not letting white men divide us
We would easily win any fight

But they knew Malcolm they knew
That's why I died first and then you
To keep us apart and embroiled in chaos

Well now it's time we went back
Cuz I'm tired of seeing our folks on crack
While Bush robs our Arab brothers of oil

We need a revolution of the minds
We need to make see those living blind
Help this generation before it's lost

Well how do we do that my brother
Does it start with the father and mother
Plant knowledge in the garden to fertilize the soil

Easier said my Christian King
When the parents only want material things
And work too hard to raise their child

That's why the village needs to return
So all kids can live love and learn
And you can accompany me on my next Hajj

Bukrah En shallah and not ma fi quais
I mean god willing tomorrow and not bad things
My Arabic hasn't been used for a while

We speak from the heart and listen with our soul
We reach out to Jesse and al to help take control
And hope young black men want to lead the charge

Brother Malcolm there's still a chance
The deejay hasn't called last dance
Someone will certainly heed our call

Dear Martin I certainly believe
That the dreams we share they'll strive to achieve
Or this once great nation is doomed to crumble and fall

For One Night

Justice can never be done when comparing the stars to you
Almost impossible to measure your beauty, but I'll try anyway
Sweet princess, be my queen
And we can rule the kingdom of love and happiness
If only for one night, let me please you to no end
Say the word and your wish shall become reality
Bathe in the light of my heart, dance to the rhythm of our love
Oblivious to the rest of the world
Open your heart and i promise to protect it with my life
Keeping it safer than my own
Erase the doubts and replace them with conviction
Remove the fears and see the promise of a better tomorrow in my eyes

Good Die Young

Angels walk amongst us every blessed day
Touching our lives in subtle unnoticed ways
Until that angel leaves our presence
Revealing the trueness of God's life lessons

The Good Die Young
For they are God's angels
Showing each of us how precious life is
Showing each of us how special life is

Do we miss their smile, their touch? Of course
But if we truly loved them,
their souls will live on within us

God Bless Them...

Insomnia

Sleepless nights and endless days

When will you bring solace to my soul

I pine away as time, our time passes by

Waiting for the day we are no longer apart

Your absence gnaws away at me like a cancer

Conceived in my mind, traveling through my body at an uncommonly rate

Attempting to overtake my heart

But our love fights it

Hope keeps it at bay

And yearns for the sight of your delectable silhouette

Each passing day

Your letters appease me but for only that short sweet moment

When your words race through my mind

Intertwining our thoughts

Returning me briefly to the happy days

Of when you and I would court

Lay me down to sleep and awaken me my love

Only when you have retuned to my side

Let me not know how much longer I must endure this punishment

This horrible exile.

Okay

Sometimes things don't go my way.

Times when the hand I'm dealt makes me feel like I'll always be in the hole.

I think about the situation and how I could effect a change.

How I could do it a little different

You can imagine what this does to my mind

Racing like the hare, when the tortoise should be my guide

But then you take my hand

You smile at me like the first time our eyes ever met.

And you tell me those magic words that bring me back to reality.

Baby, it will be Okay.

Revolution

We need a revolution. The time has come to cultivate the seeds planted by the Brother Malcolm, the Reverend King, the Honorable Mr. Garvey. The future of our present relies on the awakening of the minds and souls of our past. Activism and unity, lessons taught by the Architects must be passed down to the babies. It's on our generation to halt this slide into acceptable negligence by those designated to protect and serve. To cease the frustrated outcry of the youth who think they'll never live to see 21. We need a revolution to create an environment of encouragement, Ummah, importance, and confidence for the little ones. We need a revolution to replace the old ways of thinking, to bring accountability and safety to our communities. To show them that Black Lives Matter and Black Girls are Magic. And when the revolution comes, will you stand and be counted? Will you? I hope so...

Starlight

a memory is all I have
a beautiful one to cherish forever
a vision I have seen only in my dreams

perfection is a rarity
something to be prized and honored
raised high above so that all may see

it came to me one august night
clear as the cloudless sky
bright as Orion's star

penetrating my subconscious mind
making me instantly realize
I will always know who you are

a thousand angels sang arias
in every language known to man
praising you for your virtues

a thousand faeries flew around

twinkling so bright
that only your beauty could shine thru and then you spoke
words I will always know
fore they have been seared into my mind

you said I am your soulmate
the man of your dreams and reality
the man you have sworn to find

you seek me in my dreams
a beacon to my heart
a guiding light in the dark

so I sleep, hoping you can find me
I nap to bring you closer
my dream love, my shining star

The Message

This woman sits
Watching
Thinking
Wondering what words are flying off my fingertips
What thoughts are being digitally transferred
She has a look on her face
Like she knows these words are about her
And in a way she is right
In a way, she represents the hundreds of people who have felt the same way
People who've witnessed something divine
An interaction between God and I
Our way of instant messaging
Our way of speaking our minds
Open to all who have an insight
Closed to all who's minds can't wrap around the impossible
God inspires me everyday to write something new
Something about his people
People he loves.
Sometimes they need his help and pray to him
And he answers in his own way
He speaks to you and I directly
But in a way that only you will recognize if your heart is in it.
I look at her one last time
So I can remember the face of God's messenger today.

The Rain

The Rain has finally subsided
Allowing the sun its rightful place
A rainbow has materialized
Blazing a path through time and space

I've been caught many times in the showers
Never preparing myself for the inevitable
And when I dried I would reflect
Because the rains were so unforgettable

I would sit inside and pass the time
Watching the drops explode on the street
With each drop dying and joining the others
To become a river, a wave rushing a poor soul's feet

Sometimes the rain was too much to handle
Sometimes a sprinkle was very refreshing
Sometimes it got so hot for so long
A shower was needed to end the depression

I endured my very own personal rain
For years with no end in sight
But I guess God finally decided to act
Because my quiet storm ended last night

I'm feeling a whole lot better yu know
My Soul has a chance to finally dry out
Nearly drowning itself in misery and mirth
But never once would it try to cry out

The rain has finally subsided
Allowing the sun its rightful place
A rainbow has just materialized
Brightly blazing a path through time and space

Traveling

I slow only to glance upon her face
Her eyes draw you in
Open windows to her soul

I stop only to speak to her
Her lips profess a wisdom
A knowledge found in but a few

I wait only to bring her with me
Her heart beats with life
Playing a tune in sync with mine

I live for her and she lives for me
Two people finding life to be fun
A journey that never ends

Visions

Eyes like amber
Solid yet transparent
Opening a window to your soul

Skin soft as satin
Allowing me to race my hands freely
Never stopping, never feeling old

Lips the outlet of your wisdom
The outlet of your professions
Reminding me of your deep love

A mind as sharp as the scythe
Cutting through the rabble
Finding truth in everything told

You I can love forever
If forever your heart
Remains pure as gold.

A Woman's Hair

I love it when a woman let's down her hair
Allowing it to flow freely along
and sometimes past her delicate shoulders
And when she runs her hand thru it
it releases a sweet scent that drives me wild
Could it be that her person changed with such a subtle gesture?
Did she free her spirit
allowing her soul to play
as her dances along her neck
The beginning of the beginning
for me comes at this time
Fore she has made the first move
Waiting to see my counter..

Autumn

The capricious spirit of summer

Will soon give way to the foreboding entity that is autumn

The joy of carefree days followed by careless nights

Gives way to short coats and sweaters

Lemonade skies combined with martini nights

Turn to hot cocoa on the porch or a tall frappuccino

The summer's the time for the perfect fling

The fall's the time for the perfect love

Fore a love that can last the bitter winter

Awakening of spring, and the return of summer madness

Is a true love indeed

How Come

how come it's been a long day?
how come I need a good massage right about now?
how come if I get a good one, I'll give a good one?
how come baby oil, myrrh incense, and tea lights will set the mood?
how come Sade can play in back while you play with my thighs?
how come you can whisper the words to sweetest taboo while I close my eyes?
how come I'll moan and groan when you hit the right spot?
how come I'll sigh and gasp when you start to make me hot?
how come you can touch and tease, pull and prod
how come you can rub and squeeze, suck and bob?
how come it's so orgasmic the way your touch seduces my soul?
how come I can almost taste it as your heat begins to grow?
how come you need to straddle me when I'm on my back?
how come once you get on top, there's no going back?
how come I can feel your wetness mixing with the oils?
how come your dripping so damn much my towel's now dirty and soiled?
how come my member's throbbing now while your button beats and grows?
how come your nipples grow hard and nice while your body loses control?
how come I'm the one in charge of when this massage is done?
how come it's not gonna end for a while, I need to feel you cum?
how come touch it, taste it, share it
how come tongue it, waste it? Never!
how come cum and cum again?
how come we're done but it's not the end?

DEFAsit eduCATION

As I sit

Recalling to mind our troubled times

Something stirs in me

From where it came

I don't know

But I know it's contents

I force myself to remove

The hold your memory has on me

I push from within,

Forcing all the oxygen out

Temporary insanity or delusional anxiety

No way to tell, as the memory hits the last obstacle

A tiny barrier erected to keep in what is needed

One last gasp, and it's done

A sense of relief takes over me

I wipe my soul of the last few remnants of your reign

I discard that soiled rag, but before I go

I make sure the funkiness you have become

Is gone for good.

H2O

It's unbearable what's been going on
Almost to the point I can't breathe
Moments capture and release me like a child does a bug

Hoping that this time is the last time I feel such angst
Only the right lock will release my key
Restoring my constitution, remedying my situation
Nervous yet anxious for a sign
Yearning for that release of my essence

Capturing The Moment

It penetrates my body

Giving me immense pleasure just knowing

This force is inside me

I rock and sway with the rhythm

Hoping to stay in sync with this

Amazing thing that has me so open

I waited all day to feel this good

Anxiously counting the minutes until

This blissful experience

I lit the candles and incense

To make the moment even more intense

Because i was not operating under any false pretense

I feel my blood rushing, overwhelming my senses

Bringing me to the point I oh so love

And just like that

The moment has passed me by

Moving on to help some other hopeful soul.

Game Time

:11
Time has turned against you
Running out with mercurial speed
The crowd is roaring with delight
Enjoying its' favorite sons' slight lead

:10
Nervousness abounds
As the coach diagrams a play
Hoping his inspired creation
Will be enough to save the game

:09
Your team is down for now
But has rallied throughout the night
The coach has called a timeout
Urging you to keep up the good fight

:08
He decides to call your number
Featuring your offensive techniques
Which suddenly takes you aback
Since you ain't been an option in weeks

:07
Time to face the whole world
Or just the opposing team
A loss would be atrocious
A win would be supreme

:06
You wipe your hands of sweat
Stomach knotted in fear and joy
'Cause this is what you imagined
Since you were a little boy

:05
Ten seconds is all the time
Allotted to work your magic
A missed shot would be a shame
But a turnover? downright tragic

:04
You get the ball and eye the D
Looking for a chink in their armor
The clock is running the crowd is screaming
It's no time to have bad karma

:03
Flashing back to high school days
Where your coach taught you the basics
The time has come to use those moves
To earn your game day paycheck

:02
The fake to the left fools not a soul
As the D is set in stone
If you score the team will party all night
A miss will send you home alone

:01
You go hard right and cross back left
Leaving your man stunned in disbelief
You stop on a dime and raise for the shot
As the crowd senses eminent grief

:00
You lineup the shot and let it fly
Making sure to follow through
As the ball sails the buzzer goes off
For results check SportsCenter at 2

Lose Some

Just the other day I was waiting for you. I had it all planned out. I would pick you up and hand you the flowers I bought, give you a hug and hold your hand. Feel your blood flowing as you blush when I tell you how pretty you are. How your eyes make mine close because I can't look pure beauty straight on. I knew the restaurant was your favorite and we would have our table, the one in the corner by the wall with the picture of an angel presiding over our meal, our holy communion. Dessert would be the best part as we would feed each other some tropical delight, some tasty morsel from an island we promised to visit and watch the sunset. I could almost count the number of steps it would take to get to your place
your sanctuary
your ode to love and life
how I would be awed by the candles and incense
the paintings on the wall which all symbolized the one thing in your life I found to be greatest
but before I lost my nerve, I would have you against the wall, kissing your perfumed neck
tasting the ice cream we just finished eating
moving steadily along until we got to your bed
our canvas for what I called the art of our lovemaking
we painted so many beautiful mosaics there, it's a wonder the canvas is not full
of course if it ever did fill, we would move on to another one
but focus man!
we are almost there, almost home
I can taste it, smell it, squeeze it
she knows this and begins her game
the one I always lose because I am a fool when it comes to her
she moves me around and looks me in my eyes while she moves along my body
not touching me, but as close as one could possibly get
i am in such ecstasy I cannot move
if this were heaven, I would be its greatest angel
she moves closer and I can feel the pressure build inside me
I must control my urges if I am to win tonight!
but alas, it is as always
with her first kiss, I have come undone
I'm finished before I have even started and the game is over
maybe in the morning...

Questions

Why are we here
Naked under these sweat-filled sheets
Done for now, our ritual of pleasure

Where's the man you claim with each breath, yet deny each heartbeat
Truly unlucky fellow, or a tragic case indeed
Because him I don't envy

How do you rationalize the position you're in
Or do you enjoy being put in those positions
Releasing bits of your conscious with each powerful orgasm

Who knows of our unholy alliance besides the doorman and concierge
Am I the plumber you tell your friends about
The Messenger delivering your daily dose of Page Six

What comes now if we've been to the mountaintop already
Do I drop you off in a valley somewhere so another guy can climb your peaks
Maybe I'll just sit here and look at stars...

sigh

Showin' Off

I actualize the spiritually conceptualized style
I dramatize the saga of every consonant, number and vowel
I energize the soul to make the stanza live in love
I vaporize the bullshit leaving the truth to shine above

It's funny how the words just come
It's funny how they make a run
It's funny how they represent
It's funny how they complement

A style so familiar yet truly unique
So focused and yet diverse
Angled yet straight-forward
Cool to the touch yet warm to the heart

Bringing peace and joy to those who share in my muse
Releasing a kinetic energy to my loved ones like a power plant
Supplying friends and family with their daily dose of inspiration
Relying on God to guide my hand heart and soul in crafting touching haikus and poems

But it's not all about the love
Sometimes we need funk too
To bring us to the next level
Like a platinum Rolex with a diamond baguette bezel
Or the Benz with a name only the rich need pronounce
Or the pure uncut Colombian snow that gets you high off 1 ounce
Or some brand new Nikes no one can cop for 3 months
Or the 50 in plasma you brought so to all your friends you can front
Or the blackberry pager I use to make these here heat rocks
Or the next Common Sense joint with Kanye on the beat box
Or the grey album genius complementing the Beatles with Hov
Or my girls from Floetry making it hard for me to say No

I could go on like this forever
Cuz the words never end
But I'll stop now lucky reader
It seems there's no more ink in my digital pen

Tehya

I looked into her eyes and everything was right
I kissed her on the lips and knew she was the love of my life
I held her in my arms and sensed she felt safe
I tickled her on her sides to make a smile come to her face
I never realized I could be touched this way
Our love affair started on the very first day
At first it was all me, as she just didn't understand
But quickly it became equal as she knew I was her man
The knight in shining armor
The protector thru the storms
The comfort zone she needed
The teacher of values and norms
The love of my life and the reason I go on
The heart of my heart who needs me to be strong.

Our Island

Imagine a day when the sun warmed your body as your smile warmed my heart

When the slight breeze carried not only the fallen leaves, but the sweet scent of your perfume

When time and chance conspired to give us the luck to be together

On this day, when we were onto our own island of peace amongst a sea of chaos

Only the quiet guilt of obligations could separate us

And as we left, we could only reflect on how good it felt on that island..

Risk It All

Are you ready?
Because she might be
Waiting for the right man to enter her life
The type of guy who's brave enough to seek his fortune in her heart

Will you step out of your comfort zone?
Eschew the cheap dates and Tinder swipes
For a chance at greatness
For a chance at love?

It won't be easy, but it will be worth it
You won't be pleased right away, but the joy will soon come
She won't let you in...
Unless you know this is what you want today, tomorrow and forever

And maybe, just maybe
You fail
Maybe you
You might just fall
But you won't know if you're truly worthy of greatness
Until you decide to risk it all

Not Enough

Forgive me for I should not be writing this

I should be extolling your virtues and making promises of loving you forever

The woman who's done more for me than I've ever done for myself

Loving a guy like me in ways I never thought possible

Sacrificing time and pieces of your heart to satisfy my late night feedings

Easily, this should be your Ode to Perfection

The tribute to the greatness you extoll

There's nothing more you can do to prove you're worth your weight in diamonds

Yes, you've chosen to live your life through mine

Drawing happiness when I'm pleased

Stressing when my appetite can't be satiated

You deserve the world, the galaxy, the universe

For all you've done for me

For all you've been to me

I can only say this:

It's not enough

Your perfectly perfect in a perfect way perfection cannot be perfected

But not for me

I need something more

Something else…

Frozen In Time

That moment when we looked into each other's eyes and knew that no matter what happened, we would be alright, lives forever in my mind, frozen in time. It makes me smile again, like the goofy kid that I am, when I recall the way our arms interlocked, looping around and between each other, lost in a swirl of chocolate and caramel. How your hair was pulled into a bun, like a snake poised to spring free. The sexy do gave your almond brown eyes freedom to rule your slightly dimpled face. Those eyes I know I've gotten lost in too many times to count. That day on that street at that doorstep by that house is the soul food which sustains me when my heart flutters, and my skin feels neglected. That moment, frozen in time, when we knew we were in love.

Suddenly

Suddenly, I'm not alone

It's weird

Because I grew comfortable in my isolation

Like a warm blanket on a cold winter day

I thought this was the way my life would be

With no one to share my joys

No one to comfort my pains

Then you appeared like a subliminal fantasy

From one of my fever dreams

You showed how two could form a whole

To make a new entity

You caressed my spirit, and cajoled my soul to shine

Through the layers of gritty nothingness

Which formed on me like moss grows on a tree

Suddenly I'm alive,

Suddenly. I'm in love

Thank you

Out Of Love

I'm not in love anymore
There's no other way to say it
Time and neglect have eroded what was once a dynamic bond
I CAN live without you, your smile, your touch, your kiss
Where once your presence was sorely missed
Now i feel as if nothing is missed
I still feel your presence
like a zephyr off the ocean in June
I have endless images of your beauty
A beauty like orchids in full bloom
But my life moves ever onward
Regaining the strength sapped by our separation
Strength used to make you happy
Strength used to brighten your world
But the light faded from our romance
Like the sun setting over the pacific
Our language, once enjoys solely by us
Is now foreign to my heart and mind
You will always be a part of me
Living inside my heart forever
But it's time to let go
Time to move on

Awakening

Your touch brings me to life

Like the sun's kiss on a blooming rose

Awakening my heart from a deep slumber

Brought on by years of neglect and betrayal

Your kiss is the nourishment my soul craves and thrives on

Filling me with an energy unknown to me

Graceful are your movements

Reminiscent of the ballet I watched as a child

Your aura with a shine so brilliant

Could illuminate the way to your heart

But that is my path to find

'Fore I'm in love with you body, soul and mind.

Transconnect

My heart had something to say
It wants to express the many feelings
The joy, the happiness you bring to me each day
My heart speaks to my mind
Conveying the feelings into tangible words
Linked together for, but not always in rhyme
My mind controls my hands
The tools which transcribe these thoughts
Delivering inspired prose
For the soul of lady, child and man
My hand rules the pen
Printing my secrets with a delicate touch
Signing with love, the note to send
What began in my heart has flourished
Into a beautiful soliloquy of love
One which i will protect and nourish
Because you are a gift from above

Veteran's Day

I want to wake up to the smell of bacon,

The sound of silence as the kids have long left the nest.

Your beautiful silver streaked hair

Highlighted by the sun rays beaming through the window.

Small steps we take because youth has left our bodies.

But our spirits remain young and playful.

A kiss we share; the number has long escaped me.

But it always feels like the first one.

We've been together since before we knew we would be together.

And we'll stay together as long as Heaven has us as her own.

I grew up with you

Loved with you

Learned with you

Lived with you

With you

With

You

You Me Us

your sweet smile brightens my day
your warm embraces take me away
your charm easily enamors me
your honest opinions are of value to me

our paths have come together on this journey we call life
our souls have begun to dance under the beautiful moon-lit sky
our voices are uniting, forming a secret native tongue
our spirits scream and shout about because our fun has just begun

i'm dazzled by your honey drenched charm
i'm secure when you're wrapped in my soothing arms
i'm pleased to know you like me for who i am
i'm honored to be able to say i am your man

we can be amazing together
we can grow to become something better
we can have fun and stay focused on the prize
we can be many miles apart, yet still see the world through each other's eyes

your love is what i need to be complete
our paths is seems were destined to one day meet
i'm alone no more, 'fore i've found my eve
we can make anything happen, if we just believe

Your Voice

YOUR VOICE STRIKES A CHORD IN ME,
REWARDS ME
ENCOURAGES ME
NOURISHES ME
FULFILLS ME
REVEALS ME
CHIDES ME
SUBSIDES ME
DRIVES ME
REVIVES ME
ENLIGHTENS ME
BRIGHTENS ME
SUBDUES ME
RENEWS ME
HOLDS ME
MOLDS ME
SPANKS ME
THANKS ME
LURES ME
CURES ME
BLESSES ME…

Fresh Start Vol. 1

Fractured dreams never realized, become whole again

Reasoning deemed flawed, is suddenly sound

Emotions once dulled and subdued are now alive and fresh

Smiles, worn away by disappointment, return with the promise of a new tomorrow

Hope springs from within, after being dammed like the River Nile

Sing to me, the songs of your heart

Teach me the language of your soul

Anoint me the leader of your life

Realize your yesterday set with the Sun

Today is when our paths converged, hopefully forever.

A Week In The Life

Sunday seems kinda strange
Honey calls my name
But it's not the same

Monday my baby said to me
She was gonna leave
It's a tragedy

Tuesday she was all packed
She never looked back
My heart's slightly cracked

Wednesday I was all alone
Pleading on the phone
Baby come home

Thursday I made progress
She was still distressed
But never the less

Friday we took a long walk
Had a good talk
It was both our fault

Saturday saw her return
Our love affirmed
But I'm still concerned..

A Beginning

Is it too soon to anticipate pleasant walks along the busy avenues?
Or is it too late to curb the enthusiasm?
I seem to exude since we you graced my life?
A preordained meeting; or a carefully contrived coincidence?
Only You, I, and God know the true answer…

And There You

And my eyes lit up

Cuz there you were

The reason a man should love a woman

The reason I'm writing this poem

Amazingly beautiful, yet uncommonly shy

smiling because today was your day

As all of them are

I realize you could have any man you desire

But I want you to want me

Need me, desire me, accept me

Love me, as I do you…

Arrogant I

I thought I could have you at any time
Because I was the best thing to ever happen to you
I figured no matter what
I could always go back
Make things good like they used to be
Of course you put up a fight
Even going so far as to deny your jones for my love
I knew the passwords to unlock your body and heart
I used the right tool to confuse you long enough so I could come and go without you knowing what hit you
I took you for granted because you granted every request I had
I know I was wrong, but my pride wouldn't let me surrender my heart to you
My ego had no idea it has to concede to love
It took me months to realize this
Even more to stir the courage to tell you how I feel
Tell you I'm ready to give back everything I stole from you

So when I called you last night, looking to begin anew
I was surprised to find a different woman wearing your clothes
Who is this chick that told me no
Why do I get a message from her HeartMaster telling me my password is invalid
How could this be
I'm that dude. Don't you know
When did these changes take place
It seems I lost you to another who wasn't as foolish as I
A guy who decided he would be the man you need and want
Regardless of the day or weather
The friend you can confide in
The comforter to keep you safe
The lover to keep a smile on your face
I look at your picture one last time but I don't smile
I close my eyes and recite to myself
That man should've been me
That man should've been me
Arrogant I..

Gone

The greatest thing you ever did was leave me
I finally understand what pain feels like
I now know fear and depression are cousins
I realize the need for a hug twice a day
I sense the real meaning behind each and every word
I see the forest for what it is, a million trees in Ummah
I can now taste the bitterness of rejection
All because you were a woman's woman
You taught me how to be a man

Peace

I DON'T UNDERSTAND THE REASON YOU LIKE ME
SINCE I'VE NEVER FELT THAT WAY ABOUT YOU
I HOPE I DIDN'T GIVE YOU ANY FALSE HOPE
BECAUSE MY MOTHER SAID TO BE POLITE AND NOT RUDE
YOU CLAIM YOU SEE INSIDE MY SOUL
A PRISONER OF DESPAIR AND GRIEF
BUT WHO TOLD YOU, OH NOBLE ONE
YOU SHOULD GIVE ME THAT SPIRITUAL RELIEF?
CAN YOU NOT TELL I HAVE NO INTEREST?
CAN YOU SEE THE PAIN YOU CAUSE?
I NEED SOMEONE TO COMPLEMENT ME
NOT A PERSON WHO HAS CHARACTER FLAWS
MAYBE SOMEDAY SOMEONE WILL BE YOURS
MIND, BODY, HEART AND SOUL
BUT I KNOW IT'S NOT ME SO YOU NEED TO BE OUT
SINCE YOUR ACT IS REAL TIRED AND OLD...

Too Late

If I knew you'd be here I would have never come

I can't face you right now, no matter how many times I said I could

No matter how many times I lied to myself, believing I was over you.

Why did it take so long for me to realize you were someone special

I've been playing things over in my mind

Trying to somehow say it was your fault

But it wasn't

I can apologize until the day I die

It'll never be enough

It'll never get you back

Fuck..

Too Much

Ugh!

When will he stop bugging me girl?

Caller I'd betrays him

As he betrayed my heart

Now he wants to repair what he alone broke

How could I be just right when I wasn't enough?

The VM's during the day followed by IM's at night

Even PM's at my chill spot

For what?

So he can build up my hopes with flowery words and illusions of grandeur

Only to realize once again that I'm not worthy of his time

I could change my number, my screen name, my address, but that's way too much turmoil in my now calm world

I have to save my energy and let this fool fade away.

Emotionally Unavailable

I freed myself from the shackles of a relationship
Which had me on a downward spiral
I lost myself in the hurt, pain, and lies some call love
I dedicated too much time rationalizing instead of realizing my exit strategy
Just when I resigned myself to the mediocrity that comes with life
I stopped

I looked around and for the first time I knew I would be alright
I saw the signs the Lord laid before me
I recognized the gift he gave me
You

Your presence and words have lead me to a new level of spirituality
I am ashamed that I never believed I could pray
For someone like you to enter my life.
The aura surrounding shines like a new day, giving off a warmth I know
will secure and comfort me

But I can't be with you
My heart is at a crossroads
There's no way I could give you the love you need
I am emotionally unavailable

In time, I can gain the strength
In time I can be your equal
But you'll be gone by then
Some lucky woman's perfect find
Someone with more sense than I

Touch

I touch down and reach for the phone

Touch tones so familiar to me

I call to touch base with you

Determine when i can feel the power of your touch

But no answer, you're out of touch

I leave the message with a touch of pain in my voice

Touching my sleeve to reveal the time

I conclude the call and feel touched

Realizing you have found your way into my heart

When you touch my shoulder and smile..

Welcome Back

It's been some time since I saw your smile

I almost forgot how pretty your almond brown eyes are

I remember the way you looked at me across the room the first time

Not only did you capture my attention

You captured my heart

For reasons known only to you

We lost touch

The magic we shared diminished to almost undetectable

But it still existsI can close my eyes and see you in my mind

Feel you in my heart

Hear your voice sing through my soul

If I can hold your hand once again as we drift along the promenade

If I can kiss your soft lips as the moon sets on one of our days

If I can be your lover's rock

I would be a happy man

Welcome back

Last Dance

I left for a reason and you need to realize i can't re-engage our relationship

It's been razed to the ground, all the spirits released into the ether

Maybe we reached our full potential

And the reality of the situation has not registered in your heart

I can't continue this ritualistic dance because my feet are tired

I need to relax with Ella, bop with Coltrane, be cool with miles

Go find a new dance partner

I'm sitting this one out

Growth

Though your heart hurts
And you may not think so
Your careful love and nurturing
Have helped me to grow

The person you first met
Has long since been changed
By time and experience
Pleasure and pain

I thank you my love
Fore you showed me my life
Or better I should say
You showed me what it would be like

Our roads joined for some time
And we had a pleasant journey
But once again they must split
As fate decided it was too early

A new beginning has come
As an old ending has too
Just know that in my heart
I will always love you

Chasing Butterflies

Over the fields and through the valleys
Under the waterfalls and trees
I'll stop chasing butterflies
Because they do no good for me
Beautiful
Majestic
How could you not want to catch one
Elusive
Proud
Flying higher than I could ever reach
I need to stop chasing butterflies
Because they do no good for me
Even when I have one in hand
She stays only for a time
Then she's off on a grand adventure
Leaving me in tears far behind
They say the chase is the thing
But I'm over it
I'd rather relax with the sun on my face
Than to be chasing butterflies
Because they do no good for me

Nothing

Surprisingly, I don't have anything to write about

No heartache or love gone wrong

No mixed up feelings of neglect

Nothing really moves me

My brain has been overtaken with thoughts of practicality

Foregoing the flights into fantasy until there is want and need of such merriment

The signals I receive from God contain no flowery message

Instead they outline my plan of attack

There's not much to write so I'll stop before you get bored

Before you turn the...

Credits

Front Cover by Roxanne Tineo

Back Cover Photo by Aristotle Torres

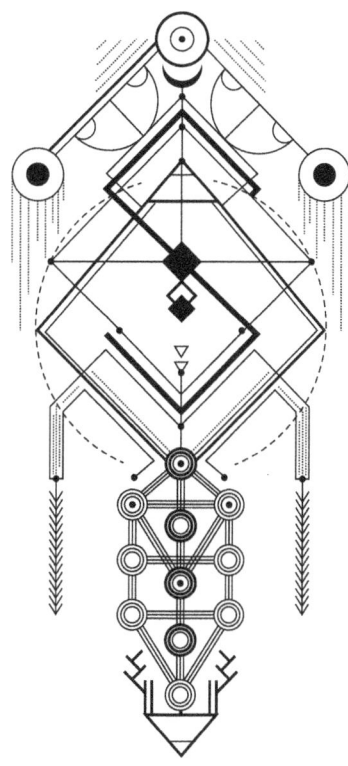

www.ingramcontent.com/pod-product-compliance
Lightning Source LLC
Chambersburg PA
CBHW031203090426
42736CB00009B/772